MAKING
YOUR OWN
GOURMET
TEA
DRINKS

Also by
Mathew Tekulsky

Make Your Own Ice Pops

Making Your Own Gourmet Coffee Drinks

The Hummingbird Garden

The Butterfly Garden

MAKING YOUR OWN GOURMET TEA DRINKS

Black Teas,
Green Teas,
Scented Teas,
Herb Teas,
Iced Teas,
and More!

Mathew
Tekulsky

*Illustrations by
Clair Moritz-Magnesio*

*Crown Publishers, Inc.
New York*

To Jane Jordan Browne

Published by Crown Publishers, Inc.
201 East 50th Street, New York, New York 10022.
Member of the Crown Publishing Group.

Random House, Inc. New York, Toronto, London, Sydney, Auckland

CROWN is a trademark of Crown Publishers, Inc.

Manufactured in the United States of America

Design by Nancy Kenmore

Library of Congress Cataloging-in-Publication Data
Tekulsky, Mathew.
Making your own gourmet tea drinks: black teas, green teas, scented teas, herb teas, iced teas, and more! / by Mathew Tekulsky.—1st ed.
p.   cm.
Includes index.
1. Tea.   2. Cookery (Tea)   I. Title.
TX817.T3T45   1995
641.8'77—dc20   94-44848
CIP

ISBN 0-517-70030-1

10   9   8   7   6   5   4   3

Acknowledgments

This is a special acknowledgment for all of the great people at Crown Publishers. No writer could ask for a better team, from editing to production to sales. I would especially like to thank Betty A. Prashker and Michelle Sidrane for their continued support. Thanks as well to Nancy Maloney, Pam Romano, and Robin Strashun for their fine efforts on my behalf. As always, I would like to thank my editor, Brandt Aymar, for his great advice and my literary agent, Jane Jordan Browne, for her continued support. Special thanks to my parents for the use of their great kitchen while I tested these recipes!

Contents

MAKING YOUR OWN GOURMET TEA DRINKS

Introduction

People have been drinking tea for thousands of years. Discovered in ancient China, this beverage spread around the world over the centuries, first to Japan, then to Europe and America. • Tea has affected every culture in which it has been introduced, from the Japanese tea ceremony to the British custom of afternoon tea. • In his classic work, The Book of Tea, *Kakuzo Okakura states: "The afternoon tea is now an important function in Western society. In the delicate clatter of trays and saucers, in the soft rustle of feminine hospitality, in*  *the common catechism about cream and sugar, we know that the Worship of Tea is established beyond question."* • Even though Okakura wrote those words in 1906, the spirit of tea not only has continued to flourish over the years, but is currently enjoying a new burst of popularity. • Today, educated tea drinkers ask their specialty tea shop for black teas with names like Assam, Darjeeling, Lapsang Souchong, and Yunnan; green teas called

Gunpowder and Gyokuro; scented teas such as Earl Grey and Jasmine; flavored black teas like Raspberry, Peach, and Mango; herbal teas such as Mint and Chamomile, as well as flavored herbal teas such as Almond,

 Cinnamon, and Lemon. • And in tearooms, restaurants, and hotels across the country, afternoon tea, at which pots of gourmet tea such as Apricot, Black Currant, Russian Caravan, Orange-and-Spice, and Vanilla tea are served alongside such standards

as English and Irish Breakfast tea, has become a popular pastime. • With this book, you will be able to bring the taste (and, I hope, the spirit) of your local tearoom right into your own home. You will learn how to make the best cup of tea possible, and you will be introduced to some creative ways of serving your tea drinks—both hot and cold. • In addition to the recipes included here, feel free to create your own gourmet tea drinks with whichever teas and other ingredients you prefer, depending on your taste. Who knows? You might come up with a few classic tea drinks of your own. • Happy brewing!

The Various Types of Tea
You Can Use

All black, green, and oolong tea (as opposed to herb tea) comes from one plant—*Camellia sinensis*, an evergreen shrub that thrives in warm, rainy climates in various parts of the world. Most of the world's tea is produced and manufactured in China, India, Sri Lanka (formerly Ceylon), Japan, and Taiwan (formerly Formosa)—although tea is also grown in such diverse places as Indonesia, Kenya, Argentina, and Russia.

Depending on where in the world it is grown, the specific variety (or subspecies) of *Camellia sinensis* that it is, and how it is manufactured, tea from different regions (and carrying different names) will feature its own characteristic taste.

For instance, Lapsang Souchong black tea from China features a smoky, full-bodied taste, while Ceylon black tea offers a more subtle, middle-of-the-road taste sensation to the drinker.

Darjeeling black tea from India has its own distinctive, delicate taste, which is known the world over, while Assam black tea, also from India, features a stronger, heavier taste.

In addition to single varieties of black tea, a number of black tea blends are popular in the tea-drinking world: English Breakfast tea is usually a blend of Ceylon and Assam teas; Irish Breakfast tea, a blend of Assam teas, has a stronger taste; Russian Caravan tea, a blend of China black and oolong teas, features the smoky taste of Lapsang Souchong; and Earl Grey tea is a blend of black teas that is scented with oil of bergamot.

Any of these black tea varieties or black tea blends (and others like them) can be used in the gourmet tea drink recipes that follow, depending on your taste.

When black tea is manufactured, it is allowed to ferment (or oxidize) before it is fired (i.e., dried by hot air); hence its black color.

Green tea is not allowed to ferment before it is fired, so it remains green. Oolong tea is allowed to partially ferment before it is fired, so its color and taste lie somewhere between that of black and green tea. Green tea and oolong tea are usually served as a single variety and are not blended the way black tea is.

Flavored (or scented) black teas have become increasingly popular in recent years, and it is now not uncommon for a gourmet tea connoisseur to order a few ounces of some black currant– or strawberry-flavored tea along with his or her Darjeeling or Ceylon tea.

Some flavored teas, such as Orange-and-Spice tea, actually have small pieces of orange peel, cinnamon, and cloves mixed in with the black tea, while others, such as Vanilla tea, actually have small pieces of vanilla bean added to them.

Sometimes pieces of dried fruit such as mango and apple are added to the tea, and in some cases, essential oils are used to flavor teas.

Jasmine tea is made by mixing green, oolong, or pouchong tea (which is slightly less fermented than oolong tea) with fresh jasmine petals during the manufacturing process, so that the tea leaves actually pick up the scent of the flowers. The same process is used with rose petals and black tea when making Rose tea. Although the petals with these teas often remain in the loose tea, they have little or no effect on the taste.

Most unflavored and flavored black teas are available in decaffeinated form. Green tea and oolong tea contain considerably less caffeine than black tea, so these types of tea are not available in decaffeinated form.

Herb teas (also called infusions or tisanes) consist of the flowers and leaves of plants other than *Camellia sinensis*. They are generally caffeine-free and are usually used in their dried form. Fresh herbs and flowers, when available, can also be used for making herb tea. Sometimes the stems, seeds, roots, and bark of various plants are also used in herb teas.

Some of the most popular herb teas include Mint, Chamomile, Rose Hips, and Hibiscus. In addition, many commercially available herb teas are flavored with pieces of fruit and various spices, as well as essential oils.

Herb teas can be blended together (as are black teas) before brewing, and they can also be grown in your garden, if you want to use them in their fresh form or dry them yourself for later use. You can also brew your herb teas separately and then mix them together in liquid form. (This is generally not done with black teas.)

Thai tea is a special type of loose tea that is flavored with star anise. It is used for making Thai Iced Tea (page 65).

In general, black, green, oolong, and herbal gourmet teas are commercially available at specialty tea shops (or tearooms), by mail order from gourmet tea suppliers, and on your local supermarket shelves. Many gourmet coffee retailers also offer full lines of tea, both for in-store purchases and by mail. Thai tea is generally available at Thai food markets across the country.

A Word About Equipment

The equipment that you will need for making a great cup of gourmet tea is really very simple and has remained virtually unchanged for hundreds, if not thousands, of years.

First, you will need a teapot—ceramic or glass is best. You may want to have both a 2-cup teapot and a 4-cup teapot on hand (or even a 6-cup teapot), depending on how much tea you plan to make at any given time. There are even 1-cup teapots available that are modeled after the traditional Chinese teapots designed for individual servings.

Some teapots come with their own built-in infusers (i.e., perforated baskets for holding the loose tea). If your teapot does not have a built-in infuser, you can use either a metal ball or spoon infuser to hold the loose tea while it is brewing in the teapot.

Be sure to fill the infuser only halfway up with the loose tea, as tea leaves expand when wet and will quickly fill up the infuser and prevent the easy flow of water through the leaves. If you want to make a larger batch of tea, simply use two half-filled infusers.

Another type of infuser that is quite effective consists of a paper filter (much like a large, open tea bag) that fits around the outside of a plastic ring with a handle. Fill the bag with tea and place the handle across the top of your teapot so the homemade tea bag hangs into the teapot and acts as a built-in infuser.

If you choose not to use an infuser and just place the loose tea in your teapot, you will need a strainer to catch the leaves that come out of the spout when you pour the tea. You can either place the strainer over your teacup or attach a strainer to the spout of the teapot.

For making Thai Iced Tea (page 65), you will need a Thai tea strainer, which consists of a cloth bag about one foot long that is attached to a metal ring. Thai tea strainers are generally available at Thai food markets across the country. (You can also use your own cloth bag.)

Two other pieces of equipment are important when it comes to making the best gourmet tea possible: an opaque, airtight container (i.e., a tin or tea caddy) for storing your tea and a tea cozy (a padded covering for your teapot that will keep the tea hot). Be sure to remove the tea leaves before placing the cozy on the teapot or your tea will overbrew.

In general, loose tea can be stored in a tea tin for six months to a year before losing some of its flavor. (Flavored teas will lose their flavor more quickly than unflavored teas.) Keep the tin in a cool, dark, dry place. Do not put it in the refrigerator, as moisture from the refrigerator will quickly ruin your tea.

How to Make the Best Cup of Hot Tea

Here are a few tips for making the best cup of hot tea possible with the equipment that you have. The following instructions apply to black, green, and oolong tea, as well as to fresh and dried herb teas, unless otherwise specified. (Since characteristics of herb teas vary so much, feel free to use more or less herb tea and shorter or longer brewing times than those specified here, depending on your taste.)

1. Always use fresh, cold water; your cup of tea is only as good as the water that is used to make it.

2. In general, you should use 1 teaspoon of loose tea (or 1 tea bag) for every 6 ounces of water that you use. Some people like to add an extra teaspoon of loose tea (or 1 extra tea bag) "for the pot" as well. It is up to you.

3. Preheat the teapot by rinsing it out with hot water, then place the tea in the teapot.

4. Bring the water to a full, rolling boil and then pour the water into the teapot. (For green tea, use water that is just off the boil.)

5. Brew the tea for 3 to 5 minutes, depending on your taste. (If you are using tea bags, you may want to brew the tea for a little shorter time than loose tea, as the larger surface area of finely chopped tea in

bags causes its flavor to be extracted more rapidly than loose tea, which generally has larger leaves.) Then remove the loose tea or tea bags from the teapot, or pour the tea through a strainer.

6. Always serve your tea immediately after you make it to retain both the heat and the freshness of the tea.

7. Be sure to clean your teapot, kettle, and all of your other tea-making equipment regularly so that tea residues or mineral deposits do not build up and ruin future cups of tea.

Making Iced Tea

There are a number of ways to make iced tea.

One method involves brewing the tea as you normally would with hot water, only use $1\frac{1}{2}$ to 2 times the amount of loose tea or tea bags as normal to account for the dilution factor of ice cubes. Pour the tea over ice immediately or after the tea has cooled to room temperature.

The *sun tea method* involves placing $1\frac{1}{2}$ to 2 times the normal amount of loose tea or tea bags in a glass container along with the normal amount of cold water that you would use for that batch of tea. Loosely cap the container and place it in the sun for 2 to 4 hours, depending on your taste. Then remove the loose tea or tea bags from the container, or pour the tea through a strainer. Pour over ice.

The *cold-water method* of making iced tea involves placing $1\frac{1}{2}$ to 2 times the normal amount of loose tea or tea bags in a container along with the normal amount of cold water that you would use for that batch of tea. Then place the container in the refrigerator for 6 to 8 hours, depending on your taste. Remove the loose tea or tea bags from the container, or pour the tea through a strainer. Pour over ice.

In general, iced tea can be stored in the refrigerator for a few days, but it is always best to make it as fresh as possible.

If you prepare your iced tea using hot water, the tea can become cloudy when chilled, depending on the type of tea that you use. (This does not affect the taste at all!) In order to make the tea more clear, simply add a little bit of boiling water to the tea and stir it around. Iced tea that is made with the sun tea or cold-water method will remain clear even when refrigerated.

A Note on Ingredients

1. When not otherwise specified, regular granulated sugar (or other sweeteners, such as honey and brown sugar) can be added to any of these drinks, depending on your taste. Many of the drinks taste fine without any sugar at all.

2. I use regular granulated sugar, but an equal amount of honey can be used as well.

3. I use whole milk, but low-fat or even nonfat milk can also be used, depending on your taste.

4. It is always best to use fresh whipped cream— generally about ¼ cup per drink.

5. I use chocolate syrup, but an equal amount of sweetened chocolate powder can be used as well.

6. I use unsweetened cranberry juice, which is available at most health food stores.

7. I use bottled or canned apricot nectar, which contains corn syrup. This will make the drink sweeter

than if you use unsweetened apricot nectar, from freshly juiced apricots.

8. In the recipes using grape juice, I usually suggest using either white or Concord grape juice, but feel free to use whichever type tastes best to you.

9. When used as garnishes, orange, lemon, lime, apple, and peach slices may be peeled or not. It is up to you. Kiwifruit and pineapple slices should be peeled.

10. Nectarine slices can be substituted for peach slices.

11. Unless otherwise specified, I use jam, but an equal amount of jelly or preserves can also be used.

12. I use cinnamon sticks, but ⅛ teaspoon of ground cinnamon can be used instead of a cinnamon stick (except as a garnish).

13. Orange-flavored herb tea may also be called Orange-and-Spice herb tea. Either will do.

14. If you wish to make more (or fewer) servings of these drinks, simply multiply (or divide) the amount of each ingredient to provide for the number of servings that you wish to make.

Hot
Drinks
Made
with
Black
Tea

Unless otherwise specified, all of the drinks in this chapter are made with freshly brewed tea that is still hot, and should be served immediately.

Pineapple Tea

This drink also tastes great when poured over ice—and the pineapple slices are a sweet treat whether hot or cold!

$1\frac{1}{2}$ *cups black tea*
$\frac{1}{2}$ *cup pineapple juice*

2 cinnamon sticks
Pineapple slices, for garnish

Combine the tea, pineapple juice, and cinnamon sticks in a saucepan and simmer over low heat for 1 to 2 minutes, stirring occasionally. Remove the cinnamon sticks and pour the mixture into 2 cups. Garnish with fresh slices of pineapple.

Serves 2

Raspberry Tea

What a delight this drink is! You get the great taste of raspberries from three ingredients—and that is before you add the whipped cream and mint!

1 tablespoon fresh raspberries
¾ cup raspberry-flavored
black tea
1 teaspoon raspberry jam

Fresh mint sprig, for
garnish
Sugar to taste (optional)
Whipped cream (optional)

Place the raspberries at the bottom of a cup and pour the tea over the raspberries. Stir in the jam and garnish with a fresh mint sprig. Add the sugar and top with the whipped cream, if desired.

Serves 1

Variations: For a Strawberry Tea, substitute 1 tablespoon sliced fresh strawberries, ¾ cup strawberry-flavored black tea, and 1 teaspoon strawberry jam for the raspberries, raspberry-flavored black tea, and raspberry jam. Proceed as directed above.

For a Peach Tea, substitute 1 tablespoon peeled and sliced fresh peaches, ¾ cup peach-flavored black tea, and 1 teaspoon peach jam for the raspberries, raspberry-flavored black tea, and raspberry jam. Proceed as directed above.

Cranapple Tea

The hot apple slices in this drink are a great treat—and they also serve as a natural sweetener.

2 cups black tea
½ cup cranberry juice
1½ cups apple juice
2 cinnamon sticks

4 whole cloves
Sugar to taste (optional)
Apple slices, for garnish

Combine the tea, juices, cinnamon sticks, and cloves in a saucepan and simmer over low heat for 3 to 4 minutes, stirring occasionally. Remove the spices and pour the mixture into 4 cups. Add sugar to each individual cup, if desired, and garnish with a slice of apple.

Serves 4

Maple Tea

Bring the taste of Vermont to your tea with the maple syrup, and add just the right spicy touch with the cinnamon.

¾ cup black tea
1 tablespoon maple syrup
¼ cup heavy cream, whipped

Ground cinnamon, for garnish

Pour the tea into a cup. Stir the maple syrup into the tea, top with whipped cream, and sprinkle with cinnamon.

Serves 1

Apricot Tea

The apricot nectar enhances the taste of this drink, which is made with one of the most popular of the flavored gourmet teas.

1 cup apricot nectar
2 cinnamon sticks
4 small strips of orange peel
4 small strips of lemon peel

3 cups apricot-flavored
black tea
Brown sugar to taste
(optional)

Combine the apricot nectar, cinnamon sticks, orange peel, and lemon peel in a saucepan and simmer over low heat for 1 to 2 minutes, stirring occasionally. Add the tea and stir to mix all the ingredients together. Remove the cinnamon sticks and the orange and lemon peel and pour 6 ounces of the mixture into each of 4 cups. Add the brown sugar, if desired.

Serves 4

Brown Sugar Tea

Brown sugar, cinnamon, and whipped cream turn regular black tea into a simple yet special treat.

½ cup milk
2 tablespoons brown sugar
1 cinnamon stick
1½ cups black tea

½ cup heavy cream, whipped
Ground cinnamon, for garnish

Combine the milk, brown sugar, and cinnamon stick in a saucepan and simmer over low heat for 1 to 2 minutes, stirring occasionally. Add the tea and stir so that all of the ingredients are mixed together. Pour this mixture into 2 cups, top with whipped cream, and sprinkle with cinnamon.

Serves 2

Cardamom Tea

Whether you serve this drink with milk, sugar, or all by itself, the exotic taste of cardamom will mix well with the distinctive taste of Darjeeling tea.

2 teaspoons loose
Darjeeling tea
¼ teaspoon cardamom seeds

1½ cups water
Milk to taste (optional)
Sugar to taste (optional)

Place the tea in a teapot. Combine the cardamom seeds and the water in a saucepan and simmer over low heat for 3 to 5 minutes, stirring occasionally. Pour this water into the teapot and let the tea steep for 3 to 5 minutes, depending on your taste. Strain into 2 cups and add milk or sugar, if desired.

Serves 2

Cinnamon Tea

The great taste of cinnamon is featured in this drink, from top to bottom—literally!

1 teaspoon loose cinnamon-flavored black tea, or 1 tea bag	¼ cup milk
1 cinnamon stick	1 teaspoon sugar
¾ cup water	¼ cup heavy cream, whipped
	Ground cinnamon, for garnish

Place the tea and the cinnamon stick in a teapot, bring the water to a boil, and pour the water into the teapot. Let the tea steep for 3 to 5 minutes, depending on your taste, and then strain (or pour) the tea into a cup. Stir in the milk and sugar and top with the whipped cream. Sprinkle with the cinnamon.

Serves 1

Ginger Tea

The taste of ginger adds a spicy accent to black tea, and the lemon adds a zesty tang.

1/8 teaspoon ground ginger (or 1/2 teaspoon peeled and sliced fresh ginger)
2 teaspoons loose black tea

1 1/2 cups water
2 teaspoons sugar
Lemon peel or fresh mint sprigs, for garnish

Place the ginger at the bottom of the teapot along with the tea. Bring the water to a boil and pour the water into the teapot. Let the tea steep for 3 to 5 minutes, depending on your taste. Pour 6 ounces of the tea into each of 2 cups. Add 1 teaspoon of sugar to each cup and garnish with small strips of lemon peel or fresh mint sprigs.

Serves 2

Spiced Cider Tea

What a delightful drink—like a tea cider! Enjoy this drink on a crisp autumn day as the leaves are falling—or anytime else, for that matter.

1/2 cup apple cider
1 cinnamon stick
2 whole cloves

1/8 teaspoon ground allspice
1/2 cup black tea

Combine the cider, cinnamon stick, cloves, and allspice in a saucepan and simmer over low heat for 1 to 2 minutes, stirring occasionally. Pour the tea into the cider mixture and stir all of the ingredients together. Strain into a mug.

Serves 1

Orange-and-Spice Tea

This milky elixir tastes like ambrosia—especially when sugar is added.

½ cup milk
1 cinnamon stick
2 whole cloves
⅛ teaspoon ground allspice
⅛ teaspoon ground nutmeg

½ cup orange-and-spice—
flavored black tea
Sugar to taste (optional)
Ground nutmeg, for
garnish (optional)

Combine the milk, cinnamon stick, cloves, allspice, and nutmeg in a saucepan and simmer over low heat for 1 to 2 minutes, stirring occasionally. Pour the tea into the saucepan and stir all of the ingredients until they are mixed together. Strain this mixture into a cup. If desired, add sugar and top with ground nutmeg.

Serves 1

Ice Cream Tea

The ice cream melts quickly, adding flavor to this drink.

¾ cup black tea

1 scoop vanilla or chocolate
ice cream

Pour the tea into a cup. Add the ice cream.

Serves 1

Mint Jelly Tea

The smoky taste of the Russian Caravan tea mixes well with the mint jelly for an exotic yet earthy drink. As a special treat, eat bits of the mint jelly as you enjoy this drink.

2 teaspoons mint jelly, or
to taste

1½ cups Russian Caravan or
another black tea

Place 1 teaspoon of jelly (or more, depending on your taste) at the bottom of each cup. Pour 6 ounces of tea into each cup and stir to the desired consistency. (You may wish to save the jelly at the bottom of the cup as a treat.)

Serves 2

Variations: Substitute orange marmalade or strawberry, cherry, raspberry, or apricot jam for the mint jelly. Proceed as directed above.

Gunpowder-Mint Tea

The delicate taste of green tea is given a light, minty after-taste in this delicious drink, which is a traditional favorite in Morocco.

> *1 teaspoon loose Gunpowder green tea, or 1 tea bag*
> *⅛ teaspoon mint extract, or 1 teaspoon fresh or dried mint leaves*
>
> *1 teaspoon sugar (optional)*
> *¾ cup water*
> *Fresh mint sprig, for garnish*

Place the tea, mint extract or mint leaves, and sugar, if desired, in a teapot. Heat the water to a boil and pour the water into the teapot. Let the tea brew for 3 to 5 minutes, depending on your taste. Strain or pour the tea into a cup. Garnish with a fresh mint sprig.

Serves 1

NOTE: You can also mix fresh or dried mint leaves in with the Gunpowder tea before brewing—½ teaspoon of each works best. Then omit the mint extract from the recipe.

Spiced Jasmine Tea

The addition of the cinnamon stick and cloves brings some new flavors to an already flavorful tea.

$\frac{1}{2}$ cup milk
1 cinnamon stick
4 whole cloves

$1\frac{1}{2}$ cups jasmine tea
Sugar to taste (optional)

Combine the milk, cinnamon stick, and cloves in a saucepan and simmer over low heat for 1 to 2 minutes, stirring occasionally. Pour the tea into the saucepan and stir to mix all the ingredients together. Remove the cinnamon stick and cloves and pour the tea into 2 cups. Add sugar, if desired.

Serves 2

Rose Black Tea

Add the flavor of rose petals to your black tea with this drink.

1 teaspoon loose black tea, or
1 tea bag
$\frac{1}{2}$ teaspoon dried rose petals,
or to taste

$\frac{3}{4}$ cup water
Sugar to taste (optional)

Place the tea and the rose petals at the bottom of the teapot. Boil the water and pour the water into the teapot. Let the tea brew for 3 to 5 minutes, depending on your taste. Strain into a cup and add sugar, if desired.

Serves 1

Mocha Tea

The chocolate and the whipped cream enhance the taste of the tea beautifully in this drink.

2 tablespoons chocolate syrup
⅓ cup milk
⅔ cup black tea

¼ cup heavy cream, whipped
Sweetened chocolate powder

Stir the chocolate syrup into the milk in a saucepan over low heat for 1 to 2 minutes, or until hot (do not boil). Add the tea and stir so that all of the ingredients are mixed together. Pour this mixture into a cup, top with whipped cream, and sprinkle with chocolate powder.

Serves 1

Tea Grog

If you want an extra taste of cinnamon in your drink, use a cinnamon-flavored black tea or a cinnamon-flavored herb tea.

2 tablespoons butter
1 cup brown sugar
1/8 teaspoon ground allspice
1/8 teaspoon ground cinnamon
1/8 teaspoon ground nutmeg
1/8 teaspoon ground cloves
12 small strips of orange peel

12 small strips of lemon peel
9 cups black tea
Milk or cream to taste
  (optional)
1 1/2 teaspoons rum extract
  (optional)

Melt the butter in a saucepan over low heat. Stir in the brown sugar, allspice, cinnamon, nutmeg, and cloves and allow the mixture to cool. Store in a sealed container in the refrigerator.

To serve, combine in each cup 1 teaspoon of the grog mixture, 1 strip of orange peel, and 1 strip of lemon peel. Add 6 ounces of tea and stir. You can also add milk or cream or 1/8 teaspoon rum extract to each cup of grog, if desired.

Serves 12

Variation: Omit the allspice and cinnamon and double the amount of ground nutmeg and cloves. Proceed as directed above.

Chai I

This traditional Indian spiced tea is as much fun to make as it is to drink—and it is quick!

2 cups water
2 teaspoons loose black tea
    (preferably Indian)
1/4 teaspoon tea masala
2 cardamom pods

2 teaspoons sugar
1/2 cup milk
1 tablespoon peeled and sliced
    fresh ginger

Combine the water, tea, masala, cardamom, and 1 teaspoon of the sugar in a large saucepan and simmer over low heat for 5 minutes. Add the milk and the rest of the sugar. Add the ginger 1 to 2 minutes after that, or when the mixture is back to a simmer. Wait for 15 to 30 seconds and then strain the tea into 2 cups.

Serves 2

NOTE: Tea masala is a premade spice mixture of ground black pepper, ground cardamom, ground cloves, and ground cinnamon. It is available at most Indian food markets; you can also create your own, depending on your taste.

Variation: To make Chai I without milk and sugar, combine the water, tea, masala, and cardamom in a large saucepan and simmer over low heat for 5 minutes. Add the ginger, wait 15 to 30 seconds, and then strain the tea into 2 cups.

Chai II

If you want to make your own *chai* from scratch, just use your own spice mixture instead of a commercially available tea masala. Please feel free to add more or fewer spices to this recipe, depending on your taste.

2 cups water
2 teaspoons loose black tea
  (preferably Indian)
2 cardamom pods
1 cinnamon stick
2 whole cloves

2 teaspoons sugar
2 black peppercorns
  (optional)
½ cup milk
1 tablespoon peeled and sliced
  fresh ginger

Combine the water, tea, cardamom, cinnamon stick, cloves, 1 teaspoon of the sugar, and the peppercorns, if desired, in a large saucepan and simmer over low heat for 5 minutes. Add the milk and the rest of the sugar. Add the ginger 1 to 2 minutes after that, or when the mixture is back to a simmer. Wait for 15 to 30 seconds and then strain the tea into 2 cups.

Serves 2

Variation: To make Chai II without milk and sugar, combine the water, tea, cardamom, cinnamon stick, cloves, and peppercorns, if desired, in a large saucepan and simmer over low heat for 5 minutes. Add the ginger, wait 15 to 30 seconds, and then strain the tea into 2 cups.

Chai III

The taste of the fennel and the cardamom make a great combination in this drink.

2 cups water
2 teaspoons loose black tea
(preferably Indian)
2 cardamom pods

¼ teaspoon fennel seeds
½ cup milk
Sugar to taste (optional)

Combine the water, tea, cardamom, and fennel seeds in a large saucepan and simmer over low heat for 2 to 3 minutes. Add the milk and 1 to 2 minutes later, or when the mixture is back to a simmer, strain the tea into 2 cups. Add sugar, if desired.

Serves 2

Variation: To make Chai III without milk, combine the water, tea, cardamom, and fennel seeds in a large saucepan and simmer over low heat for 2 to 3 minutes. Strain the tea into 2 cups.

Hot *Drinks* **Made** *with* **Herb** *Tea*

All of the drinks in this chapter are made with freshly brewed tea that is still hot, and should be served immediately.

Lemon-Mint Tea

The lemon slice is all the lemon you need in this drink to give a zesty accent to the mint tea.

$1\frac{1}{2}$ cups mint-flavored
    herb tea

2 teaspoons sugar
Lemon slices, for garnish

Pour the tea into 2 cups. Stir 1 teaspoon of sugar into each cup and garnish with slices of lemon.

Serves 2

Chamomile-Mint Tea

The refreshing mint taste complements the chamomile tea well—and the sugar and cream turn this drink into a real treat.

$\frac{3}{4}$ cup chamomile tea
$\frac{1}{8}$ teaspoon mint extract
1 teaspoon sugar

$\frac{1}{4}$ cup heavy cream, whipped
Fresh mint sprig, for
   garnish

Pour the tea into a cup. Stir in the mint extract and the sugar. Top with whipped cream and garnish with a fresh mint sprig.

Serves 1

NOTE: You can also mix fresh or dried chamomile flowers and mint leaves together before brewing—½ teaspoon of each works best in ¾ cup water. Or you can simply add equal amounts of brewed chamomile and mint tea together in the same cup. Then omit the mint extract from the recipe.

Chocolate-Mint Tea Delight

This rich, smooth drink is a great dessert all by itself. Watch the whipped cream settle on top and then slowly fall into the drink. This one is a delight!

¾ cup mint-flavored herb tea   *¼ cup heavy cream, whipped*
2 tablespoons chocolate syrup   *Sweetened chocolate powder*

Pour the tea into a cup. Stir the chocolate syrup into the tea. Top with whipped cream and sprinkle with chocolate powder.

Serves 1

Lemon-Grape Tea

This drink is also delicious when served over ice, in which case you do not need to heat up the juice before mixing it with the tea.

½ cup white or Concord grape juice
1½ cups lemon-flavored herb tea

Lemon peel, for garnish (optional)

Bring the grape juice to a boil in a saucepan over low heat. Stir the tea into the juice and pour this mixture into 2 cups. Garnish with a small slice of lemon peel, if desired.

Serves 2

Variation: For a Lemon-Apple Tea, substitute ½ cup apple juice for the grape juice. Proceed as directed above.

Blackberry-Grape Tea

The cinnamon and allspice provide a delightful accent for this robust drink. You can also use blackberry-flavored black tea instead of blackberry-flavored herb tea with this drink.

½ cup Concord grape juice
1 cinnamon stick
⅛ teaspoon whole allspice

1 cup blackberry-flavored herb tea

Combine the grape juice, cinnamon stick, and allspice in a saucepan and simmer over low heat for 1 to 2 minutes, stirring occasionally. Pour the tea into the saucepan and stir all the ingredients together. Remove the cinnamon stick and strain the tea into a large mug.

Serves 1

Orange-Apple Spiced Tea

The orange and apple slices float on the surface of this hot drink and get hot themselves—delicious!

½ cup apple juice
1 cinnamon stick
½ cup orange-flavored
  herb tea

Orange and apple slices,
for garnish

Combine the apple juice and cinnamon stick in a saucepan and simmer over low heat for 1 to 2 minutes, stirring occasionally. Add the tea and stir all the ingredients together. Remove the cinnamon stick and pour the mixture into a mug and garnish with slices of orange and apple.

Serves 1

Cinnamon Tea Punch

The combination of the apple juice and the apricot nectar makes this drink special—along with the cinnamon, cinnamon, cinnamon!

> 1 cup apple juice
> 1 cup apricot nectar
> 2 cinnamon sticks
> 2 cups cinnamon-flavored
>   herb tea
>
> Ground cinnamon, for
>   garnish (optional)

Combine the juice, nectar, and cinnamon sticks in a saucepan and simmer over low heat for 1 to 2 minutes, stirring occasionally. Add the tea and stir to mix all the ingredients together. Remove the cinnamon sticks and pour the mixture into 4 mugs and sprinkle with ground cinnamon, if desired.

Serves 4

Hibiscus-Apple Tea

This healthy elixir combines the earthy taste of apples with the flowery taste of the hibiscus—and the tastes complement each other perfectly.

½ cup apple juice
1 cinnamon stick
½ cup hibiscus tea

Sugar to taste (optional)
Lemon peel, for garnish (optional)

Combine the apple juice and cinnamon stick in a saucepan and simmer over low heat for 1 to 2 minutes, stirring occasionally. Pour the tea into the saucepan and stir all the ingredients together. Remove the cinnamon stick and pour the tea into a cup. Add sugar and garnish with a small slice of lemon peel, if desired.

Serves 1

Hibiscus-Honey Tea

The hibiscus, honey, and lemon peel blend together perfectly in this tangy yet sweet drink.

*1 teaspoon dried hibiscus
  flowers, or 1 tea bag of
  hibiscus tea
2 whole cloves*

*³⁄₄ cup water
1 teaspoon honey
  Lemon peel, for garnish*

Place the hibiscus flowers or tea bag and cloves at the bottom of a teapot. Heat the water to boiling and pour the water into the teapot. Let the tea brew for 3 to 5 minutes and then strain or pour the tea into a cup. Stir the honey into the tea and garnish with a small slice of lemon peel.

Serves 1

Cold *Drinks* **Made** *with* **Black** *Tea*

Unless otherwise specified, all of the drinks in this section are made with cold brewed tea. In order to account for the dilution factor of ice cubes, you should brew the tea using $1\frac{1}{2}$ to 2 times the amount of loose tea or tea bags as normal. Then store the tea in a sealed container in the refrigerator.

Orange-Apple Iced Tea

This delightful drink uses two of our favorite fruits, along with two of our favorite spices.

4 teaspoons loose orange-and-spice–flavored black tea, or 4 tea bags
1 cinnamon stick
4 whole cloves

$1\frac{1}{2}$ cups water
Ice cubes
$\frac{3}{4}$ cup apple juice
Orange slices, for garnish

Place the tea, cinnamon stick, and cloves in a teapot. Bring the water to a boil, pour the water into the teapot, and let the tea brew for 3 to 5 minutes, depending on your taste. Chill the tea and pour 6 ounces of the tea over ice in 2 tall glasses. Pour 6 tablespoons of the apple juice into each glass and garnish with slices of orange.

Serves 2

Black Currant–Apple Iced Tea

The black currant and apple tastes complement each other
well in this drink—and the apple and orange slices *look* good,
too!

½ cup black currant–flavored
* black tea*
½ cup apple juice

Ice cubes
Apple or orange slices, for
garnish

Mix the tea and apple juice together and pour over ice in a
tall glass. Garnish with apple or orange slices, depending on
your taste.

Serves 1

Apricot Iced Tea

The apricot and cranberry tastes mix together well in this punchlike drink—and the orange slice adds just the sweet accent the drink needs.

3/4 cup apricot-flavored
   black tea
2 tablespoons apricot nectar
2 tablespoons cranberry juice

Ice cubes
Sugar to taste
Orange slice, for garnish

Mix the tea, nectar, and juice together and pour over ice. Add sugar and garnish with a slice of orange.

Serves 1

Raspberry-Mint Iced Tea

Raspberry and mint provide a rich treat.

3/4 cup raspberry-flavored
   black tea
Ice cubes
1/8 teaspoon mint extract

1 teaspoon sugar
1/4 cup heavy cream, whipped
Fresh mint sprig, for
   garnish

Pour the tea over ice in a large glass. Stir in the mint extract and the sugar. Top with whipped cream and garnish with a fresh mint sprig.

Serves 1

Grape-Mint Iced Tea

The tastes of the mint and the grape go back and forth in this refreshing drink, which will cool you down on a hot summer day.

1 cup mint-flavored black tea	*Fresh mint sprigs, for*
1 cup Concord grape juice	*garnish*
Ice cubes	

Mix the tea and juice together and pour this mixture over ice in 2 large glasses. Garnish with fresh mint sprigs.

Serves 2

Cherry Iced Tea

This drink is like a cherry-flavored ice cream soda. You even get a real cherry with each serving!

*½ cup cherry-flavored
    black tea
Ice cubes*

*¼ cup cherry soda
1 scoop vanilla ice cream
Fresh cherry, for garnish*

Pour the tea over ice in a tall glass. Add the cherry soda and ice cream. Garnish with a fresh cherry.

Serves 1

Peach Tea Punch

The apple and grape juices bring out the flavor of the tea in this drink. Enjoy it under an umbrella on a hot summer afternoon.

*2 cups peach-flavored
    black tea
½ cup apple juice
½ cup Concord or white
    grape juice*

*1 cup ginger ale
Ice cubes
Fresh peach slices, for
    garnish*

Mix the tea, juices, and ginger ale together in a pitcher and pour this mixture over ice in 4 tall glasses. Garnish with slices of fresh peach.

Serves 4

Lemon Tea Punch

For lemon lovers, this drink is a real treat!

*1 cup lemon-flavored
black tea
Ice cubes*

*½ cup pineapple juice
½ cup lemon-lime soda
Lemon slices, for garnish*

Pour the tea over ice in 2 tall glasses. Stir the juice and soda into the tea and garnish with slices of lemon.

Serves 2

Passion Fruit Tea Punch

The orange and lime slices add their own distinct flavors to the tea, while the kiwi and pineapple slices provide tropical fruit treats that you can enjoy while you are drinking this refresher.

¾ cup passion fruit–flavored black tea
Ice cubes
¼ cup carbonated water (optional)

Sugar to taste (optional)
Orange, lime, pineapple, and kiwifruit slices, for garnish

Pour the tea over ice in a large glass. Add the carbonated water and sugar, if desired, and garnish with the slices of fruit.

Serves 1

Variation: For a Mango Tea Punch, substitute mango-flavored black tea for the passion fruit–flavored black tea. Proceed as directed above.

Tea Crush

The sweet-sour taste of the orange and lemon juices in this drink is a classic combination—and the orange and lemon slices add just the right touch. Serve this one right away, while it is still frothy.

*¾ cup English Breakfast or
    another black tea
1 tablespoon lemon juice
1 tablespoon orange juice
½ cup crushed ice*

*Sugar to taste
Ice cubes
Lemon and orange slices,
    for garnish*

Mix the tea, juices, crushed ice, and sugar in a blender for 15 to 20 seconds, or until smooth. Pour over ice in a tall glass and garnish with a slice of lemon and a slice of orange.

Serves 1

Banana Tea Blend

This drink is a great pick-me-up—like a snack. Serve it right away, while it is still frothy.

$\frac{1}{2}$ *cup black tea*
$\frac{1}{2}$ *cup milk*

$\frac{1}{2}$ *peeled and sliced banana*
Whipped cream (optional)

Mix all the ingredients except the whipped cream in a blender for 15 to 20 seconds, or until smooth. Top with whipped cream, if desired.

Serves 1

Variation: For a Banana-Chocolate Tea Blend, add 1 tablespoon chocolate syrup to the recipe. Proceed as directed above.

Strawberry Tea Shake

The flavor of the tea combines with the flavor of the ice cream to create a great summer afternoon treat.

$\frac{3}{4}$ *cup strawberry-flavored black tea*
2 scoops strawberry ice cream

Sliced fresh strawberries, for garnish
Whipped cream (optional)
Ice cubes (optional)

Mix the tea and the ice cream in a blender for 15 to 20 seconds, or until smooth. Pour into 2 tall glasses and garnish with sliced fresh strawberries. Top with whipped cream and pour over ice, if desired.

Serves 1

Variation: For a Peach Tea Shake, substitute peach-flavored black tea, peach ice cream, and slices of peeled fresh peach for the strawberry-flavored black tea, strawberry ice cream, and fresh strawberries. Proceed as directed above.

Vanilla Tea Shake

The nutmeg adds a great aftertaste to this drink and the whipped cream tops it off beautifully. Serve this one right away, before it has time to settle.

½ cup vanilla-flavored black tea	⅛ teaspoon vanilla extract
2 scoops vanilla ice cream	⅛ teaspoon ground nutmeg
	¼ cup heavy cream, whipped

Mix all the ingredients except the whipped cream in a blender for 15 to 20 seconds, or until smooth. Pour the mixture into a glass and top with whipped cream.

Serves 1

Vanilla-Orange Tea Shake

Serve this fluffy drink immediately.

*¾ cup vanilla-flavored
black tea
2 scoops vanilla ice cream*

*2 tablespoons orange juice
¼ cup heavy cream, whipped
Orange slice, for garnish*

Mix the tea, ice cream, and orange juice in a blender for 15 to 20 seconds, or until smooth. Pour into a tall glass, top with whipped cream, and garnish with a slice of orange.

Serves 1

Hot Green Tea Float

The subtle taste of the green tea comes through as the ice cream melts into this drink—delicious!

*3 scoops vanilla or green tea
ice cream*

*¾ cup freshly brewed green
tea, still piping hot
Whipped cream (optional)*

Place the ice cream in a tall glass and add the tea. Top with whipped cream, if desired.

Serves 1

Thai Iced Tea

Bring the taste of Thailand to your palate with this classic recipe.

2 tablespoons loose Thai tea
(page 15)
¾ cup water

2 tablespoons sugar
Ice cubes or crushed ice
¼ cup half-and-half

Bring the tea and the water to a boil in a saucepan and simmer over low heat for 3 to 5 minutes, depending on your taste. Strain the tea through a Thai tea strainer (page 18) into another container and stir the sugar into the tea. Pour the tea over ice in a tall glass immediately, or after the tea has cooled to room temperature. Top with the half-and-half.

Serves 1

Variations: For a really rich drink, substitute heavy cream for the half-and-half and proceed as directed above. You may also omit the cream altogether.

Cold
Drinks
Made
with
Herb
Tea

Unless otherwise specified, all of the drinks in this section are made with cold brewed tea. In order to account for the dilution factor of ice cubes, you should brew the tea using 1½ to 2 times the amount of loose tea or tea bags as normal. Then store the tea in a sealed container in the refrigerator.

Lemon-Apple Iced Tea

This drink mixes the tangy taste of lemon with the sweet taste of the apple juice.

¾ cup lemon-flavored herb tea
¾ cup apple juice
Ice cubes

½ cup carbonated water
Lemon and apple slices, for
garnish

Mix the tea and juice together and pour over ice in 2 tall glasses. Add carbonated water and garnish with slices of lemon and apple.

Serves 2

Lemon Iced Tea

This drink really packs a punch—a citrus delight!

¾ cup lemon-flavored
herb tea
Ice cubes

1 teaspoon lemon juice
1 teaspoon sugar
Lemon slice, for garnish

Pour the tea over ice in a tall glass. Stir the lemon juice and sugar into the tea and garnish with a slice of lemon.

Serves 1

Lemon-Lime Iced Tea

This purple punch will really hit the spot on a hot summer day!

2 cups lemon-flavored
herb tea
1 tablespoon lemon juice
1 tablespoon lime juice
1 cup Concord grape juice

1 cup ginger ale
Ice cubes
Sugar to taste (optional)
Lemon and lime peel,
for garnish

Mix the tea, juices, and ginger ale together in a large pitcher. Pour over ice in 4 tall glasses. Add sugar, if desired, and garnish with lemon and lime peel.

Serves 4

Almond Iced Tea

This drink is refreshing and thirst-quenching, yet it could still be a dessert in itself!

2 cups almond-flavored herb tea	Ice cubes
1 cup milk	½ cup heavy cream, whipped
2 teaspoons sugar	Sliced almonds, for garnish

Mix the tea, milk, and sugar together and pour over ice in 2 tall glasses. Top with whipped cream and garnish with sliced almonds.

Serves 2

Raspberry Tea Punch

Enjoy this drink under a veranda or in a gazebo.

½ cup raspberry-flavored herb tea	¼ cup carbonated water
2 tablespoons white grape juice	Sugar to taste
2 tablespoons cranberry juice	Fresh raspberries, for garnish
Ice cubes	

Mix the tea and juices together and pour over ice in a tall glass. Add the carbonated water and sugar and garnish with fresh raspberries.

Serves 1

Raspberry-Apple Iced Tea

The raspberries and slices of apple float on the surface of this delightful, punchy drink—and they taste great, too!

1 1/2 cups raspberry-flavored herb tea
1/2 cup apple juice
Ice cubes

1/2 cup carbonated water
Sugar to taste (optional)
Raspberries and apple slices, for garnish

Mix the tea and juice together and pour over ice in 2 tall glasses. Add the carbonated water and sugar, if desired. Garnish with fresh raspberries and slices of apple.

Serves 2

Rose Iced Tea

Bring the taste of roses into your glass with this drink!

*½ teaspoon dried rose petals,
   or to taste*
¾ cup water
Ice cubes

¼ cup carbonated water
Sugar to taste (optional)
*Sliced fresh strawberries, for
   garnish*

Place the rose petals at the bottom of the teapot. Boil the water and pour the water into the teapot. Let the tea brew for 3 to 5 minutes, depending on your taste. Strain into a cup and cool to room temperature. Pour over ice in a tall glass and add the carbonated water. Stir the sugar into the tea, if desired, and garnish with sliced fresh strawberries.

Serves 1

Chamomile Iced Tea

The ethereal taste of chamomile tea is enhanced beautifully by the apple and grape juices in this drink.

½ cup chamomile tea
2 tablespoons white grape juice
2 tablespoons apple juice

Ice cubes
Grapes and apple slices, for garnish

Mix the tea and juices together. Pour over ice in a large glass and garnish with grapes and slices of apple.

Serves 1

Orange-Grenadine Iced Tea

The slice of lime adds a nice accent to this drink.

2 tablespoons grenadine
1½ cups orange-flavored herb tea
Ice cubes

½ cup carbonated water (optional)
Lime slices, for garnish

Stir the grenadine into the tea and pour this mixture over ice in 2 tall glasses. Add the carbonated water, if desired, and garnish with slices of lime.

Serves 2

Cinnamon-Cranberry Iced Tea

The cinnamon, cranberry, and pineapple tastes mix well in this tart, earthy drink.

½ cup cinnamon-flavored
   herb tea
¼ cup cranberry juice
½ cup pineapple juice

Ice cubes
Sugar to taste
Cinnamon stick, for
   garnish

Mix the tea and juices together and pour over ice in a tall glass. Add sugar and garnish with a cinnamon stick.

Serves 1

Cranberry-Cherry Iced Tea

The cranberry and cherry tastes blend beautifully to create a punchlike drink.

½ cup cranberry-flavored
   herb tea
Ice cubes

¼ cup cherry soda
Sugar to taste (optional)
Fresh cherry, for garnish

Pour the tea over ice in a tall glass. Add the cherry soda and sugar, if desired, and garnish with a fresh cherry.

Serves 1

Hibiscus-Grape Iced Tea

Hibiscus and grape are marvelous tastes, both separately and in conjunction.

    1 cup white grape juice   *½ cup carbonated water*
    1 cup hibiscus tea   *Orange slices, for garnish*
    Ice cubes

Stir the juice into the tea and pour over ice in 2 large glasses. Add carbonated water and garnish with slices of orange.

Serves 2

Hot Mint Tea Float

Enjoy the ice cream as it melts into this drink!

3 scoops mint chocolate chip
   ice cream
¾ cup freshly brewed mint-
   flavored herb tea, still
   piping hot

¼ cup heavy cream, whipped
   Sweetened chocolate powder

Place the ice cream in a tall glass and add the tea. Top with whipped cream and sprinkle with chocolate powder.

Serves 1

Mint Tea Float

Chocolate, mint, and whipped cream—all in one drink! What could be better?

¾ cup mint-flavored herb tea
2 tablespoons chocolate syrup
2 scoops vanilla ice cream

¼ cup heavy cream, whipped
   Sweetened chocolate powder

Pour the tea into a tall glass. Stir the chocolate syrup into the tea, add the ice cream, and top with the whipped cream and chocolate powder.

Serves 1

Variation: Substitute 2 scoops of chocolate ice cream for the vanilla ice cream and chocolate syrup. Proceed as directed above.

Orange Tea Crush

The sherbet mixes with the tea to form a slushy orange- or lemon-flavored drink.

> *¾ cup orange-flavored herb tea*   *½ cup crushed ice*
> *½ cup orange sherbet*

Mix all the ingredients together in a blender for 15 to 20 seconds, or until smooth. Pour into a tall glass.

Serves 1

Variation: For a Lemon Tea Crush, substitute lemon-flavored herb tea and lemon sherbet for the orange-flavored herb tea and orange sherbet. Proceed as directed above.

Almond-Vanilla Tea Shake

Almond and vanilla make a great combination of tastes—a real treat!

½ cup almond-flavored herb tea
2 scoops vanilla ice cream

Whipped cream (optional)
Sliced almonds, for garnish (optional)

Mix the tea and ice cream together in a blender for 15 to 20 seconds, or until smooth. Pour the mixture into a tall glass. Top with whipped cream and garnish with sliced almonds, if desired.

Serves 1

Peach-Yogurt Tea Shake

This drink can also be made using peach-, strawberry-, or raspberry-flavored black tea. Enjoy!

*½ cup peach-flavored
    herb tea*
½ cup peach yogurt

1 tablespoon honey
Peach slices, for garnish
Ice cubes (optional)

Mix the tea, yogurt, and honey together in a blender for 15 to 20 seconds, or until smooth. Garnish with fresh slices of peach. (You can also pour this drink over ice, if desired.)

Serves 1

Variations: For a Strawberry-Yogurt Tea Shake, substitute strawberry-flavored herb tea and strawberry yogurt for the peach-flavored herb tea and peach yogurt. Proceed as directed above and garnish with sliced fresh strawberries.

For a Raspberry-Yogurt Tea Shake, use raspberry-flavored herb tea and raspberry yogurt. Proceed as directed above and garnish with fresh raspberries.

Gourmet
Tea
Drinks
with
Liquor

In addition to the liquors mentioned in this chapter, feel free to add your own combination of liquors to whichever teas you prefer, depending on your taste. The recipes in this chapter are for hot and cold drinks made with black tea and herb tea. Salut!

Hot *Drinks* Made *with* Black *Tea*

Rum-Cider Tea

The rum adds a special accent to this mulled cider tea—great for sitting in front of a fire on a cold winter day.

½ cup apple cider
1 cinnamon stick
2 whole cloves
⅛ teaspoon ground allspice

½ cup black tea
2 tablespoons rum
Orange and lemon peel, for garnish

Combine the cider, cinnamon stick, cloves, and allspice in a saucepan and simmer over low heat for 1 to 2 minutes, stirring occasionally. Pour the tea into the saucepan and stir all the ingredients together. Strain the mixture into a cup, add the rum, and garnish with a small slice of orange and lemon peel.

Serves 1

Rum-Brandy Tea

A spirited tea, this drink needs no embellishments. It is fine just as it is.

¾ cup black tea   1 tablespoon brandy
  1 tablespoon rum

Pour the tea into a cup. Stir the rum and the brandy into the tea.

Serves 1

Anisette Tea

The licorice taste of the anisette mixes well with the mint in this drink.

¾ cup black tea   Fresh mint sprig, for
  2 tablespoons anisette liqueur   garnish
¼ cup heavy cream, whipped

Pour the tea into a cup. Stir the anisette into the tea, top with whipped cream, and garnish with a fresh mint sprig.

Serves 1

Orange-Spice Tea Delight

The orange-and-spice tea combines beautifully with the red wine, cinnamon, and brown sugar to produce a hot mulled punch.

¼ cup red wine
1 cinnamon stick

¾ cup orange-and-spice—
flavored black tea
1 tablespoon brown sugar

Place the wine and the cinnamon stick in a saucepan and simmer over low heat for 1 to 2 minutes, stirring occasionally. Pour the tea into the saucepan and stir in the brown sugar. Pour into a mug.

Serves 1

Hot *Drinks* **Made** *with* **Herb** *Tea*

Chamomile-Brandy Tea

Whether you use the brandy or the crème de menthe, your chamomile tea will never be the same.

¾ cup chamomile tea
1 tablespoon brandy
Sugar to taste (optional)

Lemon peel, for garnish
(optional)

Pour the tea into a cup. Stir the brandy into the tea. Add sugar and garnish with a small strip of lemon peel, if desired.

Serves 1

Variation: For a Chamomile-Crème de Menthe Tea, substitute 1 tablespoon crème de menthe for the brandy and omit the sugar and lemon peel. Proceed as directed above.

Grand Marnier Tea

Enjoy a special after-dinner treat as you sip the Grand Marnier through the whipped cream—incredible!

¾ cup orange-flavored herb tea
2 tablespoons Grand Marnier liqueur

¼ cup heavy cream, whipped
Grated orange peel, for garnish

Pour the tea into a cup. Stir the Grand Marnier into the tea, top with whipped cream, and sprinkle with grated orange peel.

Serves 1

Amaretto Tea

The great taste of amaretto bursts into your mouth with this drink.

6 tablespoons amaretto liqueur
1½ cups almond-flavored herb tea

½ cup heavy cream, whipped
Ground almonds, for garnish

Stir the amaretto into the tea in 2 cups. Top with whipped cream and sprinkle with ground almonds.

Serves 2

Galliano Tea

Lemon and Galliano are made for each other—wow!

¾ cup lemon-flavored herb tea
2 tablespoons Galliano
   liqueur

Lemon peel, for garnish

Pour the tea into a cup. Stir the Galliano into the tea and garnish with a small strip of lemon peel.

Serves 1

Mint-Cocoa Tea

Two of our most popular liqueurs are blended together in this drink—great for warming you up on a cold winter evening.

¾ cup mint-flavored herb tea
1½ tablespoons crème de cacao
1½ tablespoons crème de menthe
¼ cup heavy cream, whipped

Sweetened chocolate powder
Fresh mint sprig, for
garnish

Pour the tea into a cup. Stir the crème de cacao and crème de menthe into the tea. Top with whipped cream and chocolate powder and garnish with a fresh mint sprig.

Serves 1

Cold *Drinks* Made *with* Black *Tea*

Lemon Tea Punch

This drink is great for the beach, a picnic at the park, or a Fourth of July barbecue.

½ cup lemon-flavored
  black tea
2 tablespoons lemon juice
2 tablespoons orange juice
¼ cup ginger ale
¼ cup champagne

Ice cubes
Sugar to taste
Orange, lemon, or
strawberry slices, for
garnish

Mix the tea, juices, ginger ale, and champagne together and pour over ice in a tall glass. Add sugar and garnish with slices of orange, lemon, or strawberry.

Serves 1

Cocoa-Mint Tea Shake

Drinking crème de cacao and crème de menthe through whipped cream is about as close to perfection as you can get.

<table>
<tr><td>½ cup black tea</td><td>1 tablespoon crème de menthe</td></tr>
<tr><td>1 scoop vanilla or chocolate ice cream</td><td>¼ cup heavy cream, whipped</td></tr>
<tr><td>1 tablespoon crème de cacao</td><td>Fresh mint sprig, for garnish</td></tr>
</table>

Mix the tea, ice cream, crème de cacao, and crème de menthe in a blender for 15 to 20 seconds, or until smooth. Top with whipped cream and garnish with a fresh mint sprig.

Serves 1

Mint Julep Tea

Feel free to use mint-flavored herb tea as well with this drink.

<table>
<tr><td>¾ cup mint-flavored black tea</td><td>Sugar to taste</td></tr>
<tr><td>Crushed ice</td><td>Fresh mint sprig, for garnish</td></tr>
<tr><td>2 tablespoons bourbon</td><td></td></tr>
</table>

Pour the tea over ice in a tall glass. Stir in the bourbon and the sugar. Garnish with a fresh mint sprig.

Serves 1

Cold *Drinks* Made *with* *Herb* Tea

Red Wine–Tea Punch

This tangy, winy punch is perfect for a party. Enjoy!

1 cup orange-flavored herb tea	½ cup carbonated water
1 cup red wine	Ice cubes
½ cup orange juice	Sugar to taste (optional)
½ cup cranberry juice	Lemon slices, for garnish
½ cup apple juice	

Mix the tea, wine, juices, and carbonated water together in a pitcher and pour over ice in 4 tall glasses. Add sugar, if desired, and garnish with slices of lemon.

Serves 4

Iced Crème de Menthe Tea

Cool, minty, and refreshing, this drink is a real winner!

1½ cups mint-flavored
herb tea
Ice cubes
¼ cup crème de menthe

½ cup heavy cream, whipped
Fresh mint sprigs,
for garnish

Pour the tea over ice in 2 tall glasses. Stir the crème de menthe into the tea, top with whipped cream, and garnish with a fresh mint sprig.

Serves 1

Index

Conversion Chart
Equivalent Imperial and Metric Measurements

American cooks use standard containers, the 8-ounce cup and a tablespoon that takes exactly 16 level fillings to fill that cup level. Measuring by cup makes it very difficult to give weight equivalents, as a cup of densely packed butter will weigh considerably more than a cup of flour. The easiest way therefore to deal with cup measurements in recipes is to take the amount by volume rather than by weight. Thus the equation reads:

1 cup = 240 ml = 8 fl. oz.   ½ cup = 120 ml = 4 fl. oz.

It is possible to buy a set of American cup measures in major stores around the world.

In the States, butter is often measured in sticks. One stick is the equivalent of 8 tablespoons. One tablespoon of butter is therefore the equivalent to ½ ounce/15 grams.

Liquid Measures

Fluid ounces	U.S.	Imperial	Milliliters
	1 tsp	1 tsp	5
¼	2 tsp	1 dessertspoon	10
½	1 tbs	1 tbs	14
1	2 tbs	2 tbs	28
2	¼ cup	4 tbs	56
4	½ cup		110
5		¼ pint or 1 gill	140
6	¾ cup		170
8	1 cup		225
9			250, ¼ liter
10	1¼ cups	½ pint	280
12	1½ cups		340
15		¾ pint	420
16	2 cups		450
18	2¼ cups		500, ½ liter
20	2½ cups	1 pint	560
24	3 cups		675
25		1¼ pints	700
27	3½ cups		750
30	3¾ cups	1½ pints	840
32	4 cups or 1 quart		900

Solid Measures

U.S. and Imperial Measures		Metric Measures	
ounces	pounds	grams	kilos
1		28	
2		56	
3½		100	
4	¼	112	
5		140	
6		168	
8	½	225	
9		250	¼
12	¾	340	
16	1	450	
18		500	½
20	1¼	560	
24	1½	675	
27		750	¾
28	1¾	780	
32	2	900	
36	2¼	1000	1
40	2½	1100	
48	3	1350	
54		1500	1½
64	4	1800	
72	4½	2000	2
80	5	2250	2¼
90		2500	2½
100	6	2800	2¾

Equivalents for Ingredients

granulated sugar—caster sugar
half and half—12% fat milk
heavy cream—double cream
light cream—single cream
vanilla bean—vanilla pod
zest—rind